The Classroom
Cultivating Kingdom Dancers

Joshua Forbes

Joshua Forbes

Copyright © 2017 Joshua Forbes

All rights reserved.

ISBN-13: 978-1977989833

CONTENTS

	Acknowledgments	4
	About Me	6
	Introduction	9
1	The Question	13
2	Spiritual	27
3	What Stops the Flow of the Anointing	32
4	How to Stay in the Spirit	39
5	Natural	47
6	Be a Servant Leader	57
7	Class Dismissed	62

ACKNOWLEDGMENTS

First I would like to give honor to my Lord and Savior Jesus Christ who has changed my life. He has never left me, He has always been with me, even when I didn't know it. I want to thank him for allowing me to be free in every area of my life. There have been times where I thought I would never get free in certain areas of addiction, habits, wrong mindsets, situations but His love for me is something I cannot explain.

I would like to thank my Gorgeous, Gentle but Strong, Smart, Intelligent, Demon-Chasing Wife, Toya Forbes. Without her, I would not be at the place where I am now in my life and you probably would not be reading this book if she hadn't pushed me into finishing it and getting it done! I am truly Blessed and Highly Favored of God to have this woman in my life. I thank her for accepting me as her husband, and I pray that I will continue to be the man that she believes and knows that I am.

To my Amazing, one-of-a-kind Father and Mother Raymond and Sandra Forbes. You are the best parents any son could have. Thank you for raising me up in the ways of the Lord and trusting that God's purpose and plan would be fulfilled in my life. I honor you and thank you for your Love, Support and the never ending unwavering Faith you have concerning me.

About Me

Born and raised in Queens, New York, Joshua Forbes came to Oklahoma at the age of 17 and got inspired to dance by a church Hip Hop group and fell in love with dance instantly. After joining the Victory church dance team and danced for two years, he then attended and graduated as the first Male Graduate at Oral Roberts University with a B.S. in Dance Performance. Other accomplishments include the following:

Music Videos: Performed as one of the lead dancers in National Recording artist Hanson Brothers music video called "Thinkin Bout Somethin" and "Give a Little," also performed with music artist Fedel in "Walk it like I'm Changed."

Experience: Joshua Forbes has been a guest performer in the Tulsa Opera and has worked with some of the top artists in the Dance Industry from the Step Up Movie Series, So You Think You Can Dance and America's Best Dance Crew. He also opened up for Biker Boy shows, Hair shows, Festivals, Church Conferences, performed and choreographed in Modeling shows. Special guest performances in live theatre productions

"Hairspray," "Super Sweet," "Dhadkah," "Rasa," "Shakti," and "Sangama."

He has been on Good Morning Memphis T.V. show and toured with his dance crew "The Production" as special guest performers on the World of Dance stage around the country. (W.O.D. is one the biggest urban competition company in the World and are now partners with NBC).

Commercial Personality: Video ad for the Bell House Dance/Art Cooperative, Simple Simons Pizza, National Oil Co. Baker Hughes "Think Process Safety," Fine Airport Parking "Detail Shop FineDango," and Naples Flatbread and Wine Bar Commercial.

Choreographed 3 Commercials: Car Country "You're Approved," Car country "Green Zone" and Rogers Auto Group "Bing Bang in Shelby."

Instructor: He has taught dance for 10 years in Tulsa, Oklahoma.

Companies worked with/hired by: Tulsa Ballet, Tulsa Opera, World of Dance, Life-Time Fitness, Parkside Psychiatric Hospital and Clinic (StressBuster Program), Camp Strong at Shepherd's fold Ranch sponsored by Saint Francis Health System, Jenks High School, Tulsa Hope Academy, Dove Dance School, Jenks Dance Academy, Broken Arrow Dance Co., Destined2Dance Co., Centerstage and South Tulsa Dance Co.

Director Experience: Assistant Director of the first NBA Flash-mob for the Oklahoma City Thunder in 2014, Director of "Word in Action" Theatre Company 2014 and Director for Engaged2Dance Co. 2015.

Currently: Adjunct Professor at Oral Roberts University Dance Department, Co-Director of Transformation Church Dance Team, and has started his own company Forbes Entertainment with his wife, Toya Forbes.

Introduction

I grew up in a Christian home with one sister and no brothers. Dad was the assistant pastor of a church in Brooklyn, New York, and Mom coordinated events at the church. We had Monday night prayer, Thursday night Bible study, and Sunday service. Sunday service consisted of morning service, Sunday school, and then night service from 11am - 9 pm. My sister is five years older than me, so there came a time where she went off to college to Oral Roberts University.

As time went by, my parents decided they wanted to move to Tulsa, Oklahoma right as I'm entering into my junior year of high school. Now why in the world would we do that? I mean I was born and raised in New York. My parents are originally from Jamaica, but have lived in New York for almost twenty-two years with no major problems or issues, so why the sudden change?! Next thing I know, we're in Tulsa, and it was a major culture shock for me—big time.

Eventually, I finished my junior and senior year of high school at Victory Christian Center and attended Oral Roberts

University as well. I got to college not knowing what I wanted to do, who I wanted to be, or what made me happy, etc. My mom was a nurse, and my sister was going to school to become a nurse, so naturally everyone was looking to see what career in the medical field was I gonna choose. I knew I wanted to do something else, just wasn't sure what yet. I started praying about it and asked God what I was supposed to do. Before I knew it, the answer came through a very clear cut dream: Dance.

Then all of a sudden, I was in chapel one day at school, and the administration announced that a new Dance program was starting that semester for students who wanted to pursue a career in Dance. I said to myself, "This cannot be happening right now." I had already developed a love for dance when I got to Oklahoma, joined a dance team to keep me occupied, so for all of this to be happening at once, it had to be a sign, and I took it! Four and a half years later, I graduated with a B.S in Dance Performance, and I was off to do what I love.

For some reason, even though I started my own dance group out of college, I still didn't fully understand why God wanted me to choose Dance as a major. Where did this talent of dance all of a sudden come from? Nobody else in my family dances, and I wasn't dancing in New York before I came to Tulsa—so what is the plan here? How could God use dance? What was my purpose for dancing? As I began to ask these questions, I realized that I wasn't the only one. Many people, younger or older, in different walks of life still ask the question, "What do I do with my talent and gift?"

As I began to study God's Word—getting understanding and revelation through different books written by great men—God began to show me who I am, what my purpose was and what everyone should be doing with the gifts and talents He has given them. Everything is about the King and his Kingdom, so everything that has been given to us is to be used for the benefit of his Kingdom.

This book is mainly split up into two sections: the Spiritual and the Natural. A lot of dancers today especially Christian dancers have many questions that I feel the church has not answered. Many of them have no direction. They're often coming up against resistance by parents, church members, peers, and they get discouraged and give up the passion God put inside them to get a 9 to 5 job all because of a lack of knowledge and understanding. As a dancer, one of the things God is calling me to do is to Cultivate Kingdom Dancers and let them know the reason why they dance. How does dancing build the Kingdom? What does a Kingdom dancer look like from a spiritual and natural point of view. How are we different from any other dancer? This book answers many unanswered questions individuals may have concerning their purpose!

Please understand, this book is not just for dancers alone, but for any person who has questions and wants to understand God's original plan in the most simplistic way. It can be in the areas of Entertainment, Education, Medicine, Government, etc. The basic principles apply to everyone no matter what field you are in.

CHAPTER 1

THE QUESTION

Mr. Forbes: Ok class, don't forget your assignment. I need to see at least four 8 counts of your choreography on Monday morning before we go into our new lesson. Our topic we'll be discussing is how to be a "Kingdom Dancer." Don't procrastinate over the weekend!

(school bell rings)

Josh: Mr. Forbes, can I talk to you for a sec?

Mr. Forbes: Sure, what's up?

Josh: Well, I been a little frustrated lately. I don't know what I want to do with my life. I mean, I love to dance, but some people don't really recognize dancing as a real career. As a man, I need to be the "provider, the money maker," so I need to get a "real career" like being a Doctor, Lawyer, Banker, Physical Therapist etc. because apparently, "there's no money in dance."

Mr. Forbes: Wait. What?

Josh: Hey, that's what they're saying, Mr. Forbes.

Mr. Forbes: Well, I have some friends right now making ten grand a month just off of dance videos they created on YouTube, Instagram, Vine. Not to mention all the other Commercials, Corporate Events, Choreography gigs, TV shows and Movies they do. Why you think your assignment for the week is four 8 counts of Choreography? I'm training you guys to make your own stuff, to be creative and be dope at your craft so that you can be the next Choreographer for SYTYCD, go on tour with the next hottest artist or get a movie deal! People perish for a lack of knowledge and understanding, Josh.

Now I will advise you not to have dance as your only source of income, but as you begin to identify your other gifts and natural talents God has given you, you need to turn those gifts into streams of income. Of course, there is budgeting, saving and managing the money you have coming in properly, but I would think beyond just being a dancer, but think as an Entrepreneur, an Entertainer, a Business owner. What about investing your money in other things that will allow you to make residual income while you sleep. The point is you should have multiple streams of income working for you and all your natural gifts and talents are those streams.

Just be led by the Spirit and just take one day at a time and don't worry! Matthew 6: 25-34 talks about if God clothed the lilies of the field which are here today and gone tomorrow, how much more will he take care of you who are more valuable to him then they. "For he has a plan to prosper us and not harm us; to give us a future and a hope"(*Jeremiah 29:11*). All you have to do is study to show yourself approved (*2 Timothy 2:15)*, which means work hard on your craft and trust God with all your heart and believe that He will open doors for you that no man can shut *(Revelations 3:8)*. But remember you have to "Seek first the Kingdom of God and his righteousness and all these things will be added unto you *(Matthew 6:33)*.

Most people when they read that scripture don't really know or understand what that really means so let me translate:

Seek: Search for, try to find, give diligent dedication, explore, understand, learn and study.

First: Make top priority, something of the highest value, placed above everything else

The Kingdom of God: the sovereign rulership of the King, His territory/domain and what his Will, Purpose, Desires, and Intentions are.

And His Righteousness: Also study and learn the Terms, Conditions and Requirements of God's Kingdom and Government. How to stay in right relationship, right positioning and right alignment.

All These Things: Everything that pertains to Life and Godliness that people are in constant search for or trying so hard to obtain: Physical needs, Social needs, Emotional needs, Psychological needs, Financial needs, Security, Self significance and Self-worth, Clear Direction, Purpose etc.

Will Be Added: Will automatically be given, received without toil or hard labor.

To You: Placed in your hands.

Josh: Dang Mr. Forbes, you really know your Word, huh?

Mr. Forbes: Lol. I grew up on the King James version but lately been looking through the Living Bible. But hey, you've got to know your Word in this day and age with so much crazy stuff going on in the world. Government corruption, preachers teaching false doctrine in the pulpit, false prophets running around the place acting like they hear something, laws being passed that have no business being passed. You have to have that Word hidden in your heart because soon, they are going to try and take all the Bibles away just like they did in the schools.

You have got to know your Word so well to the point that God begins to give you a tongue and such wisdom that nobody can deceive you, resist you or trap you (*Luke 21:15*). That way in the last days you will be one of the few people that will be Bold and Unashamed of the Gospel of Jesus Christ (*Romans 1:16*), and stand up for righteousness when everyone else starts to run and follow the One who calls himself the Christ (*Luke 21:8*). Anyway, we're getting way off subject lol.

Josh: Naw, you good, Mr. Forbes. You just inspired me to get back in my Word, because you cold wit the scriptures. You're not talking that religious stuff either. You just spitting that truth for real.

Mr. Forbes: That's what's up, man! Hey, just follow me as I follow Christ *(1 Corinthians 11:1)*.

Josh: Oh, of course, because you know Jesus is the only way, the truth, and the life and no one can go to the Father but through Him *(John 14:6)*.

Mr. Forbes: OK OK, I SEE YOU!!!!

Josh: Aww they not ready for me, Mr. Forbes. Lol.

Mr. Forbes: Lol.

Josh: (brief moment of silence takes place)

Josh: I don't want to take up too much of your time, Mr. Forbes, but what's this new topic we gonna be talking about?

How to be a Kingdom Dancer, right?

Mr. Forbes: Yes, that's correct.

Josh: Well, I know we start the topic on Monday, but I wouldn't mind getting a head start on the lesson and meditating on it over the weekend. It may help with some questions I have...

Mr. Forbes: Ok, talk to me about these questions. I got time!

Josh: Well, I know God has a plan for me, I know I have to trust him with my life, but I wish I knew everything right now...

Mr. Forbes: Don't we all! lol

Josh: What is my purpose? What should I be doing with dance? What does it mean to be a "Kingdom Dancer"? I don't get it...

Mr. Forbes: Well, before we can begin to answer all these questions, first we must define both terms separately.

Kingdom - the sovereign rulership and governing influence of a king over a territory. Impacting that territory with his Will, Purpose, and Intentions, producing a culture and lifestyle that reflects the king's character and nature.

Dancer -is a person who uses movement, gestures, and body language to portray a character, story, situation, or abstract concept to an audience through music.

The next thing you will ask is, "So how does this relate to each other? How does this help me understand my purpose?" Well, in order to understand your purpose, you have to understand the Creator of your purpose. Why he put us on this earth in the first place, and why he even gave you the gift of dance? It all goes back to the beginning.

Josh: Okaaay...?

Mr. Forbes: Myles Munroe couldn't have said it better when he said, "God, who existed before all things, created an invisible world which initiated the concept of "ruler." Another word for ruler is "king." God called this invisible world/realm or domain "heaven," thus becoming the king over the domain, "heaven." So the first kingdom was called the invisible "Kingdom of God" or "Kingdom of Heaven."

Josh: Ok. That makes sense!

Mr. Forbes: Right, So Who is the King?

Josh: God.

Mr. Forbes: What is the first kingdom or territory called?

Josh: The Kingdom of Heaven

Mr. Forbes: God wanted to extend his Kingdom of Heaven to Earth, and he wanted us to rule it, manage it, develop it and maintain order for Him as representatives or vice-regents! *(Genesis 1:26-28, Psalm 115:16)*.

(Moment of silence with a puzzled look on Josh's face)

Mr. Forbes: You have more questions, huh? Well, ask away…

Josh: What is God's original purpose for man?

Mr. Forbes: God created mankind to assist him in bringing the culture of Heaven to Earth; to allow his Will, Purpose and Desires to be easily understood and recognized. In other words, He wanted an extension of himself on Earth-for His nature and character to be clearly seen through our actions, words, deeds, activities and lifestyle in our everyday culture and society.

Josh: So what you're saying is God wants us to represent him and what his kingdom stands for in everything we do? To allow his Will and Desires-even his Character and Nature to be seen by the people we come into contact with? For them to see God through us and in us?

Mr. Forbes: Yes!!!!

Josh: Well, what characteristics does God have that we are to follow and show?

Mr. Forbes: Well, the very first thing to understand is that God is Love—which means God is patient, kind, never jealous or envious, never boastful or proud, never haughty or selfish or rude. God does not demand His own way. God is not irritable or touchy. God is never glad about injustice, but rejoices whenever truth wins out *(1 Corinthians 13:4-6)*.

God is Love and without love, we do not really know Him. Once we get to know God and give him control of our lives, then certain characteristics of God's Spirit are produced: Love, Joy, Peace, Patience, Kindness, Goodness, Faithfulness, Gentleness, and Self-Control *(Galatians 5:22, 23)*.

Josh: Ok, OK...Then, What is the first step in getting to know God and developing his character and nature?

Mr. Forbes: So glad you asked. Well, accepting Him into your heart is the first step. "For if you confess with your mouth that Jesus Christ is Lord and you believe in your heart that God has raised Him from the dead, then you will be saved" *(Romans 10:9)*.

Now that you have accepted Christ into your life, you can begin to develop a relationship with Him by spending time with Him, talking to Him on a daily basis (prayer) and reading His Word. Before you know it, you start to "love God with all your heart, soul, mind, strength" *(Mark 12:30)* and your desires by default become submitted to God's desires for your life and what he wants you to do.

One of God's main desires and commandments to all who follow him is the Great Commission: "Go into all the World and make other followers (disciples), baptizing them in the name of the Father, Son and Holy Spirit and teaching these new followers to obey all the commands I have given you *(Matthew 28:18-20)*.

God not only wants you to enjoy this new friendship, abundant life, and free gift of salvation, but He wants other people to know Him too, so they can know what He has done for them. He wants us to spread the "Good News." What is the Good News? "For God so loved the world that he gave his only Son so that whoever believes in him should not perish but have eternal life" *(John 3:16)*.

See, in the beginning, sin entered into the entire human race by a man called Adam because he disobeyed God when he was told not to eat the fruit from the tree of Good and Evil (*Genesis 2:15-17; Genesis 3*).

Adam's one sin brought the death penalty to all mankind. Not fair, I know! But through God's grace and mercy and through Jesus obedience and sacrifice by dying on the cross, He brought forgiveness and salvation to all (*Romans 5:12-19*).

Josh: So….if we are to represent God by our actions and lifestyle in our culture and society and go into the world and share the good news to everyone we meet, then what does that mean for a dancer? What is my culture or arena of influence?

Mr. Forbes: Let's define culture, shall we?

Culture is a particular society, group, place or time that has its own beliefs, customs, way of life, or art. The culture or world we live in is known as the Entertainment World. Within this world, the art form of our culture that we have the most influence in is "Dance."

So according to the Great Commission, we are to go into the world of Dance & Entertainment and share the "Good News" of salvation to everyone we come in contact with. We are to represent Christ and let God's nature and character be clearly seen through our actions, lifestyle and activities.

The way we can do this is by using dance, which is a gift God has given us, as a tool to infiltrate that culture. We are like secret agents of change.

It's not about how talented or skilled you are. It's not about who you know, how many connections or even how much money you have; it's all about lives being changed—and that, is our mission and purpose as "Kingdom Dancers."

CHAPTER 2

SPIRITUAL

Mr. Forbes: Now that we understand the purpose for us having the gift of Dance, which God has given us, the next question you might ask is what makes us different from all the other dancers?

-Yes, we have accepted Christ into our lives.
-Yes, we are going into the world and sharing the Gospel.
But what will truly give us the upper hand? What will distinguish us from anyone else? The answer is *"The Anointing."*

To Anoint- to pour on, smear all over, or rub into. (Ex: David whom God anointed with oil on his head) (1 Samuel 16:13).

The Anointed- Symbolic of blessing, someone handpicked, empowerment; chosen one. A person was anointed for a special purpose; to be king, prophet (Ex. Jesus was anointed by God with the Holy Spirit to spread the Good News and free those who were been held captive by sin) *(Isaiah 42:1)*.

The Anointing- The Anointing is God's spirit and power, on us and in us, by the Holy Spirit (*Luke 4:18*).

Josh: Well, how do I get this Anointing?

Mr. Forbes: By receiving the baptism of the Holy Spirit with the evidence of speaking in tongues. Jesus was baptised and received the Holy Spirit (*Acts 10:38; Matthew 3: 13-17, Mark 1:9-11*), and so did the disciples in the upper room before they started doing ministry (*Acts 1:4; 2:1-4*). So the anointing is God's Spirit and Power working in us and through us by the Holy Spirit for His service and work he wants us to do on the Earth (*2 Corinthians 4:7; Acts 1: 7,8;* Mark 16:17,18; *1 John 2:27; Matthew 3:11*).

The word "Christ" means "the Anointed one." The same Anointing that came upon Jesus to preach the gospel, heal the sick, and set the captives free is available to you (*Luke 4:18,19*). "I can do ALL things through "the Anointed one and his Anointing" which gives me strength (*Philippians 4:13*).

If you are in Christ and have been "Born Again," which simply means you have given up your old way of doing things and have chosen to repent and turn away from your old lifestyle and follow after Jesus, then there is an anointing for everything God has called you to do, no matter how small or big the task may be. This same anointing can heal your body, help you succeed financially, make you the top dancer in your region, and empower you to live a holy and set apart life.

Josh: Wow, that's tight. So the Holy Spirit helps us complete our assignment on Earth?

Mr. Forbes: Right, It's the Holy Spirit that helps us in every aspect of our lives. He's our best friend that will walk with us through life and give us the ability to stand out, be a light in this Industry of Dance and empower us to prosper in our mind, body, spirit and soul. Let me quickly show you some back up Scriptures:

-Acts 17:28 says, "In Christ, we live and move and have our being."

-John 6:38 says, "For I have come here from heaven to do the Will of God who sent me, not to have my own way."

-John 5:19 says, "The Son can do nothing by himself. He does only what he sees the Father do because whatever the Father does, the Son does also."

-Isaiah 42:1 says, "See my servant, whom I uphold; my Chosen One (anointed one), in whom I delight. I have put my Spirit upon Him. He will reveal justice to the nations of the world.

-Galatians 2:20 says, "I have been crucified with Christ: and I myself no longer live, but Christ lives in me. And the real life I now have within this body is a result of my trusting in the Son of God."

Now here's the next thing. The devil doesn't want us to find out who we are, the anointing we carry and what we are called to do because once we do, the anointing will begin to increase as we start walking into the fullness of who God has called us to be. In return, people will start surrendering their lives over to God's Kingdom instead of the Devil's Kingdom because of us. So the enemy's job is to stop us at any cost. So now let's pretend you're the devil....

Josh: Wow, Seriously??!!?

Mr. Forbes: Lol, just for a second…

You know that this power that flows through sold out believers can break every chain, and destroy the yoke of bondage off of people's lives, and you know that true believers carry this anointing wherever they go especially if they spend time in His presence. The more you spend time in his presence and in worship, the stronger the anointing on you becomes. What would be your strategy of attack against this believer, this so called "Kingdom Dancer"? What question would you ask yourself and your demons?

Josh: The question I would ask is, "How can we slow them down? How can we separate them from having fellowship with God? How do we stop the flow of this anointing?"

Mr. Forbes: EXACTLY!!!!!! The answer to that is....SIN!

CHAPTER 3

WHAT STOPS THE FLOW OF THE ANOINTING?

Christ died on the cross so that we no longer have to be a slave to our sinful desires. That's why we have to keep renewing our minds daily—so our spirit man can remain strong and so we don't fulfill the lust of our flesh. We have to allow God to clean us up from every sin that would entangle us and keep us from his anointing fully operating in our lives. How can I help you with something if I'm dealing with the same stuff behind closed doors? We have to be healed healers and delivered deliverers for God's power to move frequently and easily through us. We have to live a lifestyle of Holiness and Purity before God, if not then we open the door to the enemy.

1 Corinthians 6:9-10 is very clear on some of the sins that can keep us forever separated from God's kingdom and what the Devil uses to slow us down and keep us in bondage:

Fornication- Is sexual intercourse between two unmarried people *(Ephesians 5:3, 1 Corinthians 6:18-20, Romans 6:13)*

Adultery- Sex with a married person other than his or her own spouse (1 Corinthians 7:2).

Homosexuality- Having romantic sexual attraction or behavior between members of the same sex or gender *(Romans 1: 25-27, Leviticus 18:22)*.

Idol Worship- Giving honor and showing respect or having love for an object, image, or idea *(Matthew 6:24)*.

Thief/Robber- The taking of someone's property without permission or consent, to take by force illegally *(Ephesians 4:28 Leviticus 19:11)*.

Drunkard/Drunk- Being in a temporary state in which one's physical and mental faculties are impaired by alcoholic drink, a person who is habitually or frequently drunk *(Proverbs 20:1, Ephesians 5:18)*.

Slanderers- Talking about someone with intent to damage their reputation *(James 4:11, Exodus 23:1)*.

Gossip- Is a person who habitually reveals personal or sensational facts about others, whether true or false *(Proverbs 20:19, Ephesians 4:29, Ex. 23:1)*.

Gluttony- A person who over-indulges and over-consumes food, drinks or wealth items *(1 Corinthians 6:13)*.

Josh: Wow...I've been doing most of those things not even realizing it was a sin! That's Whack...

Mr. Forbes: It's all good; that's why we have to read God's Word daily and find out what He says concerning the life He wants us to live. We can find the answer to every situation we go through in the Bible. Remember we have to represent Christ in everything we do so that means we are the light sent to the world. We give people hope and show them a different path that leads to love, peace, joy, wholeness, restoration, healing and manifestation of every good thing but doing it God's way.

So bitterness, unforgiveness, pornography, masturbation, anger, hate, lying and even having impure thoughts can stop the consistent flow of God moving in our lives and getting us to where we need to be.

Josh: Man, I don't know if I'm ready for all this. I'm pretty messed up then. How can God use me if I've done half of the stuff the Bible tells us not to do. I'm not like you, Mr. Forbes.

Mr. Forbes: Well, let me say this...No one is sinless, that's clearly stated in Romans 3:10-12. You think I just popped out of the oven perfect? Lol, that's a negative! There is also a difference between falling short and practicing sin, making sin a lifestyle and just expecting God to be ok with it....ah NO!

We all fall short of his glory and even our righteousness is still like filthy rags to God. If we walk with God and continue to commit and submit ourselves to Him, He will give us the power to resist the devil, and He must flee. If you have done these things in the past or even if you are doing them right now, it's all good. You must understand the true Gospel.

Creflo Dollar breaks it down like this: "The too good to be true news is the Undeserved, Unmerited Favor of God, which is the Grace of God. Your righteousness is not based on going from good deed to good deed! Your Good deed did not make you a righteous person or get you saved! When you accepted Christ into your life, Jesus made you Righteous just because you believed in the finished work that He did on the cross for you.... It is your Faith and Belief in Him!! That's it!!

When Jesus died on the cross, He took away past, present and your future sins, and technically everybody's sins were in the future because none of us were born yet! Lol under the Agreement of Grace, you get what you Don't Deserve"!! All he requires and desires is for us to have a relationship with him. Read Romans 3:21-29; it will explain some things more in detail.

Josh: So if God took care of sin on the cross, why can't I keep on sinning?

Mr. Forbes: Well, for one, you can't serve two masters. Second, if you continue to practice sin as your lifestyle, then Satan becomes your Father and you really are not a part of the family of God because by your actions, you have chosen who you want to serve and obey *(1 John 3:7-10)*. Once Christ died for you, sin no longer has power or control over you.

Just think of the symbolism of getting baptized. When you were lowered in the water, your old sin-loving nature was buried with Him and just like Jesus when he rose again from the grave, you too came up from the water, and entered into new life to enjoy! Romans chapter 6 explains that really well. You should take a look when you have time.

Josh: Man, I just feel so....

Mr. Forbes: Stop...

"For there is no guilt or condemnation to them who are in Christ Jesus, who walk and seek after the spirit and not after the flesh" (*Romans 8:1*). For if any man be in Christ he is a new creature, old sinful desires are passed away and behold all things have become new (*2 Corinthians 5:17*).

See you have to understand, Jesus knew we couldn't do this on our own; that's why he came down to save us and be our strength when we are weak. He knew we would need Him. So it is not by our strength, might or ability that we can resist the enemy but it is by Jesus Christ and His Power; through the Holy Spirit, we are able to be more than conquerors.

So cheer up, Psalms 103:12 says "As far as the east is from the west so shall He remove our sins from us." Don't worry about anything; instead pray about everything. God's got this, and he's got you! Instead of focusing on doing right or wrong, just keep your eyes focused on Him who is the author and finisher of your faith, and He'll do the rest.

CHAPTER 4

HOW TO STAY IN THE SPIRIT

Josh: I got you...I feel better now! I remember a scripture that says "Faith comes by hearing the Word of God" *(Romans 10:17)*. Thank you, Mr. Forbes. That devil was trying to make me feel like there was no hope for me, that God can't use someone like me because of my past, so I might as well keep doing what I been doing and stay down this road, but that's a LIE!

If God's word says I'm a new creature, then there's nothing else to talk about. I am CHANGED! All I have to do is make a continual decision to follow after Christ, repent, turn from my ways, humble myself under God; he will exalt me, lift me up and take away everything that is not like Him.

Mr. Forbes: There you go! You better resist that devil.... Speak boldly...Speak Out Loud and tell that Devil who's Boss...

Josh: Yeah, for no weapon formed against me shall prosper and every tongue that rises up against me will fall *(Isaiah 54:17)*.

Mr. Forbes: That's right; life and death is in the power of the tongue *(Proverbs 18:21)*. Speak Joshua! Speak!

Josh: I am the head and not the tail, above and not beneath *(Deuteronomy 28:13)*. Greater is He that lives in me then He that is in the world *(1 John 4:4)*. I am Strong in the Lord and in the Power of His might *(Ephesians 6:10)*, and I do NOT have the spirit of Fear but of Power, Love and a Sound mind *(2 Timothy 1:7)*.

Mr. Forbes: Aw snaps, Spirit is moving now!

Josh: I am smart, handsome, and intelligent, and I will succeed in life. Wealth and riches shall be in my house, and I can do all things through the "Anointed one and his anointing" that gives me strength; for if God be for me then who can be against me, *(Romans 8:31)*. I can and will be used by God. I forgive those who have wronged me, talked about me and those who have not believed in me; therefore, because I forgive, God can and has already forgiven me of all my sins because of His great love for me. Now, because I have a better understanding of His love I can forgive myself and let go of the past *(James 4:12)*, and

Psalms 75:7 says, "For who can judge me?" Only God can, for he has the power to put one down and raise another.

Mr. Forbes: Now, Speak who you are!!

Josh: I am the Light of the world, a city on a hill, glowing in the dark for all to see *(Matthew 5:14)*.

Mr. Forbes: WHAT IS YOUR MISSION?

Josh: To infiltrate the devil's kingdom as a secret agent using the gifts that God has given me and get people saved, set free and delivered. I will take down anything that stands in my way that does not represent God's Kingdom.

Mr. Forbes: WHAT IF YOU FAIL?

Josh: I cannot fail, for Christ says, "We may face trials, sorrows and even opposition here on Earth but Be of good cheer for I have overcome the world" *(John 16:33)*. So I will not fail my king because no one will be able to oppose me or stand against me all the days of my life, for as God was with Moses, so shall he be with me. He will not abandon me, forsake me or fail to help me *(Joshua 1:5)*.

Mr. Forbes: You sound like you're getting prideful, soldier?

Josh: No, sir 1 Corinthians 1:31 says, "He who boasts, let him boast in the Lord," so what you hear is confidence in God's ability working through me by the Holy Spirit to get the job done. I'm the man for the job and best believe every wall of Jericho that the enemy has set up to Stop me, Hinder me or Block me WILL COME DOWN! Oh Thank you Lord, for I.......ring ring.... wait....one second.....hello?

Mr. Forbes: Distraction....

Josh: Yeah, I'm still in class talking to Mr. Forbes. I'll call you when I'm out, ok cool, later. What was I about say again?

Mr. Forbes: Now, you tell me what just happened?

Josh: umm....

Mr. Forbes: The Holy spirit just took over, and you were flowing in the spirit. God was downloading revelation of who you are in Him and was about to give you something else to speak but the phone rang, and you answered. The moment you answered the connection you had in the Spirit realm got cut off immediately. So let me break this down...Spiritual Warfare 101.

The enemy saw that your faith was getting sparked by hearing me speak God's Word to you. You then started listening and meditating on it because the Word was getting down in your spirit and creating roots. Then you opened up your mouth to speak by faith and the Holy Spirit took over, and he started speaking through you even when it seemed like you didn't know what to say or what you were talking about.

Remember my question to you earlier and remember your answer? The enemy will do anything he can to distract and stop you from flowing in that anointing. Think about the timing of that "important phone call" you think that was just coincidence? There is no such thing...That was strategically planned and timed by the enemy, and you fell for it.

Josh: Wow, Mr. Forbes...I didn't see that, Wow.

Mr. Forbes: It's ok, you're still learning...You're entering into another level of Spiritual Warfare, so now you know for the next time. Do not underestimate your enemy. If he can use the simplest things to take our minds and hearts off the word of God, even for a second, then he's got us. Be always alert and vigilant for we are not ignorant of the enemies' devices *(2 Corinthians 2:11)*.

Josh: Gotcha...I'll definitely be keeping my eyes and ears open from now on! Wait...so what are some of the things I can do to stay in the spirit?

Mr. Forbes: Well, as Kingdom Dancers we always have to be...

Reading God's Word Daily

It's like food. His Word feeds, nourishes us, guides us, renews our thoughts, gives us ammunition to use against the enemy, and reminds us of his promises and so much more *(Psalms 119:105; 2 Timothy 3:16-17; 2 Timothy 2:15; Joshua 1:8)*.

Constantly Praying and Fasting

Prayer is just communicating or talking to God. It's having a normal one on one conversation all the time. Prayer also gives God access and legal right to move in our lives and situations. Fasting kills our flesh and makes our spirit man stronger. If you have a situation, problem or struggle you're dealing with and you pray and pray and for some reason it won't go away...You need to FAST! The Bible says, "This kind of demon comes out only through fasting and praying." Certain things in your life are strongholds, and that demon does not want to leave your life so you have to kill it or what I like to say, "Starve it out" *(1 John 3:21-22; Mark 11:24-25; 1 Thessalonians 5:16-18; Matthew 17:17-21)*

Worship and Thanksgiving

We have to always be grateful. Always letting God know how much you appreciate Him. We must give Him honor, thanks and praise for being who He is in our life. Thank Him for changes He has made in your life, for training you, teaching you and for saving you. Worship is also a battle tactic against the enemy. It's a form of transferring the battle from your hands into His hands and getting a flawless victory in any situation you may face *(Psalms 92:2-4; Chronicles 20:22-25; Acts 16:22-31)*.

Stay in Faith

Faith is the confident assurance that if there is something we are believing for that lines up with God's Word, then we will have it. Faith comes by hearing the Word of God, so as we feed ourselves with the Word daily, our faith grows. When our Word intake is low, then our faith becomes low, and it is impossible to please God without Faith. If our car always needs gas in the tank to keep running, then we need God's Word to keep us going, keep us growing, and keep us believing that He will do what He said He will do. Start in Faith, Stay in Faith and End in Faith...there is no other way! *(Hebrews 11:1; Romans 10:17; Mark 11:22-23)*.

Obey The Lord

Obedience is very important because God can't anoint or use people who don't listen to him. Until we live a life of consecration and full surrender to God's will and plan, then we will never walk in the full power of the anointing God has for us. Obedience is better than sacrifice *(1 Samuel 15:22-23; John 14:23-24)*.

Chapter 5

Natural

Mr. Forbes: Now that we've touched on the spiritual aspect of being a Kingdom Dancer, let's talk about the practical aspects. Seeing that we are representatives of Jesus Christ and that people see Christ through our actions, words, and deeds, we need to make sure that we carry ourselves with excellence in the field of influence we are in. We need to show that we have the following:

Character - Features and traits that form the individual nature of a person or thing, moral or ethical qualities.

Integrity - Consistency of actions, values, methods and principles; honesty and truthfulness, steadfast to a strict moral or ethical code.

Professionalism - the conduct, the skill, good judgment, polite behavior that is expected from a person who is trained to do the job well.

These things are very important because you can be the top Dancer, best Singer, most wanted Lawyer, well respected Doctor in the country, but if people can't stand being around you, or if people don't trust you, then what good does all the fame get you? So there's the Spiritual and the Natural aspect you must consider when becoming a Kingdom Dancer. Here are certain other practical things that I put into practice.

Time Management

If you're asked to be somewhere, for a job, project, gig etc, be there at least 15-30 minutes early. Show people you value their time and the opportunity given to you. Developing good time management skills will take you a long way. People who are punctual tend to have whatever they need for the next day already laid out and placed in certain specific places around the house before they go to bed the night before. Be ORGANIZED! Have your materials prepared ahead of time so you don't waste other people's time, energy, and money. Any materials, choreography, paperwork of any kind, need to be done and finished way in advance before the due date.

STOP PROCRASTINATING!

It will get you nowhere, and you will miss out on opportunities that may present themselves. Why do it later when you can do it done now, get it over with, and move on to something else important?

Be on time and End on time. Plan ahead to figure out how long you should spend on a project: teaching a class, talking on the phone, having business meetings, team mentoring etc. Learn how to value other people's time, and in return your time will be valued when you most need it. What you do to others, others will do to you. There are so many things that can be done in one day but if we have bad time management, then it will seem more like six hours in a day versus twelve hours, and most of the important things never get done.

Make a list of your daily goals each day from the smallest task to the biggest one; even some alone time needs to be added. This will ensure your days, weeks, months, and years will consistently be productive.

Listen/Communicate

Always pay attention! Don't get distracted by your peers or be a distraction to others. Don't miss out on an opportunity because you were not at the right place at the right time because you were too busy on your phone or trying to entertain that cute guy or girl standing next to you in an audition. You want to be able to listen and understand so well that you become the person that everyone else goes to if they didn't understand or didn't get all of the information.

Be an effective communicator! This sometimes means less talking and more listening. Listening well is not just understanding the words or information being communicated, but also understanding the emotion behind what the person is trying to say which will give you the ability to repeat, in a detailed matter, what needs to be done.

If you're an owner of a company, leader of a group or just getting hired for a job, always communicate with the people you are around or in charge of.

DON'T ASSUME ANYTHING!!!

Check and double check to make sure everyone understands in detail what you are thinking, what you're planning, what is required of them, where everyone should be, at what time and the list goes on. Where there is a lack of proper communication, you will usually find chaos, confusion and frustration.

Follow Instructions

If you're not listening, how can you follow the instructions that were given? No Choreographer or Producer wants to repeat themselves over and over again. Don't add to or take away from the instructions given especially if you think you know more or less than the person giving the instructions. Respectfully follow the person who is in charge. Once again, do to other people what you would want someone to do to you; so when you are the one in charge or in that leadership position, you are going to want people to follow your instructions and show you the same respect.

Quality Work

Take your time and allow the Holy Spirit to guide you in producing something so creative that people have not seen. Let your talent stand out above what everyone else is doing; go beyond your limitations and see what is on the other side. Hard work pays off in the end. Actions speak louder than words. Go the extra mile because you will be remembered for it. If you say you're going to do something, then do it. Don't always make excuses for why you couldn't do it or why you couldn't be somewhere, especially at the last second because then you become an unreliable person, and no one will want to hire you or work with you again. If you are very talented and produce great results for a client, stay Humble! Continue to work in excellence and people will pay for what you have. Your gift will make room for you *(Proverbs 18:16)*.

Attitude

Don't complain. Always maintain your Joy and Peace that only God can give. Someone might get on your last nerve, or the Choreographer might accuse you of something you didn't do. That's the perfect time to stand out from the rest and let your light SHINE! Just smile; thank him for the correction and keep on pushing. God sees all things and he is the ultimate judge. One of my mentors told me, "If you can change a situation, why get upset...if you can't change the situation, why get upset." If you're faithful in the small, God can trust you to be faithful with the big (*Luke 16:10*). Having an attitude of gratitude will get you far and will open up more windows of opportunities that you never anticipated.

Comparison\Patience

If you're on tour and someone else gets to be in front or gets picked for a specific part, so what! Let it go! Continue to work hard! Be content where you are positioned and get excited for the other person who also worked hard and got moved up. God has a plan for your life, so don't worry if you're not the leader, or haven't got picked for a specific job or gig. When it's the right time, God will open those doors for you that no man can shut! Does God not love you? Are you not his child?

As your looking and seeking for opportunities, take this time while you're waiting to study yourself. Explore all your gifts and talents and begin to discover who you are and what God has called you to do. Build Confidence, Boldness, and Courage, and be ready at all times to run through those doors when it opens. Don't compare yourself with others and ask yourself, "Why did they get that; how did that happen for them and not me"?

STOP IT!!! CHANGE YOUR PERSPECTIVE!

Think something like this: "if God can do that for them, then he can do that for me, too." If that is your perspective, then get excited for the person who got the job or promotion. It could be a test to see where your heart is, and your reaction to someone else's blessing could determine the level of your blessing. We are all God's children which means we are all the light of the world. Some people have a 40 Watt light bulb; others may have a 100 Watt bulb, but when you shine either light in a dark room, both light up the room. So don't worry about someone else's light; just work the light God gave you and when the time is right, he will elevate you. Be Patient!

It's not WHAT you know; it's WHO you know

"A man that has friends must first show himself friendly " *(Proverbs 18:24)*. Build good solid healthy relationships with people! You never know who the person is standing next to you. Never judge someone off of their appearances or background. Be kind and respectful to everyone you come in contact with. All it takes is that one person who knows somebody who knows somebody else which could set you up for life. Be led by the Holy Spirit. He will guide you to the right connections for the purpose of building the kingdom and to fulfill your destiny.

Don't Wait

Do what you gotta do. Family will procrastinate, friends will come and go, people will try and hold you back or slow you down, situations in life will tell you it's never the right time, but when God says "Move, you better Move." You don't have time to waste because there are people waiting on you to fulfill your purpose in order for their lives to be changed.

Stop making excuses why you haven't explored that new idea, started your own business, auditioned for that company or commercial. Stop blaming other people or holding on to past experiences, for why you haven't moved forward in what God has told you to do when it's really FEAR you are dealing with. God is waiting on you and your Faith to do the impossible.

Speech/Language

Ephesians 4:29; 5:4 says, "Don't use bad language. Say only what is good and helpful to those you are talking to, and what will give them a blessing. Dirty stories, foul talk and coarse jokes--these are not for you. Instead remind each other of God's goodness and be thankful." Our conversation should be so different from those around us to the point that they know that something is different about us, and they don't say certain things in your presence; they feel convicted. Let us always speak Faith and not Doubt. Remember we are to plant seeds of Life everywhere we go and it starts with your mouth.

Chapter 6

Be a Servant Leader

Servant - someone who desires to put the needs of others above their own needs and desires.

Leader - a person who leads a group, organization or country; someone who motivates, inspires and guides others toward a pre-established goal.

Be a servant leader wherever you go. You have the greater one and his anointing that lives on the inside of you. Walk in Confidence, Boldness, Courage, and Humility with no Fear! You don't need to have a position of leadership or authority over people to be a leader. For example, I remember one time during our Easter production at my church, everyone was breaking for lunch. They had two tables packed with boxes of pizza, cups, sodas, napkins, chips, plates, and people were reaching over each other trying to grab this, trying to grab that; it was chaos, and none of the main leaders were around. I thought to myself, "If I move all the sodas, cups, napkins and chips to the end of the second table and leave all the plates and pizza on the first table, and turn the pizza boxes in opposite directions to two lines instead of one line, then I think things would go much faster and smoother." So guess what I did? I took initiative and went to work! I moved everything around, got the job done, and there was peace and order. I was serving everyone to the best of my ability and as small as that may be, I became a servant leader at that very moment without the need to be recognized or acknowledged.

Leadership is influence, and if you lead with confidence, people will follow you. Use your leadership to serve others, not to be served.

Leadership Position

Your prayer life has to go to the next level if you are going to be in a Leadership Position. As my pastor would say, "saturated in prayer and bathed in Faith." You need consistent guidance and direction from the Lord on how to serve/lead with Accuracy, Boldness, and Grace. You need to also be consistently praying on behalf of the people you are leading as well because under your servant leadership, you should see them changing, growing and prospering in every area of their lives because of your prayer life and the example you set before them. Teach, Develop and Empower the leader on the inside of them and draw out the gifts, talents, and abilities that are hidden.

Delegate everything you can to people in your organization you trust or have proven to be consistent and reliable. You cannot do everything on your own! If everything is on your shoulders, you will get frustrated, burnt out fast and you will take that frustration out on the people that are the closest to you and the people you are leading which will cause DAMAGE.

Make your load lighter, and you will stand longer and stronger. Make sure your lifestyle outside of your organization is in order and reflects the nature and the characteristics of Christ every day. You don't want to give the enemy access to any area of your life because it will affect how you lead. What's on the head will fall down to your organization.

Continue to develop your leadership skills everyday so when the opportunity presents itself for you to lead, you will know what to do and how to do it!

Good Leadership is

Learning from your mistakes

Engaging with your people or organization consistently

Adjusting your methods or your way of doing things

Delegating and developing the people you're leading

Empowering others

Refusing the good for the great

Self-Evaluation everyday

Humbling experience

Influence & Initiative

Pain & Sacrifice that you must go through in order to be like Christ

Good Leadership will produce

Legacy for generations

Energy and stamina

Answers you've been seeking

Duplicates of Christ and not of yourself

Expectation of God's goodness and favor

Resources you never expected

Space & Quiet time
Help that God will send
Income and opportunities
Purpose driven life

LOVE

Love is an ACTION word. If God is love, and God lives in us, then we need to be showing the love of God all day, every day-- even to the people that don't like us, are jealous of us, lie on us, cheat, accuse us and the list goes on. Anyone can love someone when love is given back, but the true strength and maturity is when you love those that don't love you *(Matthew 5:44-48)*.

If we are to MAKE a difference we have to BE the difference in our Actions, Words, and Deeds!

CHANGE BEGINS WITH YOU!!

Chapter 7

Class Dismissed

Josh: Wow!!! That is some good stuff, Mr. Forbes! I have learned so much that I feel like I can take on the world. I'm going to be the best representative of the Kingdom I can be. Thank you for taking the time to explain and break all this down to me. See, I never had a Father, so sometimes I feel confused about some things...

Mr. Forbes: Wait, I don't understand; you talked about your parents earlier?

Josh: Well, my Dad left when I was five, and I haven't heard from him since. My mom passed away when I was sixteen, so me and my sisters are actually living with my adopted parents. My adopted Dad is cool, but he's a little older and works a lot so I'm usually by myself trying to figure things out, you know.

Mr. Forbes: I see...well how about this. Why don't you come to church with me and my wife on Sunday and meet some of the guys in the youth group. They're looking for more volunteers, and they could use someone with your skills on the dance team.

Josh: Are you serious!? That would be AWESOME!!!!

Mr. Forbes: Yeah, we'll go to the gym afterwards, play some basketball then maybe get something to eat. What's your favorite dish?

Josh: (silence)

Mr. Forbes: Josh? You ok man?

Josh: (tears run down his face) I don't know what to say, sir! I....

Mr. Forbes: You don't have to say anything. God always has a plan, a bigger plan, and he knew you needed to be in this class this semester and knew you would get curious and want to hear more about the lesson on Monday. God always works everything out for our good for them that love Him and are called according to His purpose (*Romans 8:28*).

But before we go…you have to forgive your Dad.

Josh: What? Mr. Forbes?

Mr. Forbes: I know, I know…but there are certain principles in God's Word that do NOT change for nobody. You cannot think you're going to be a representative of the Kingdom and walk around with unforgiveness. God is your Father, and He will never leave you nor forsake you and he has always been with you, but in order for you to go to the next level in God you have to let this Go!

Josh: (silence)

Mr. Forbes: God is right here with us, and all you have to do is ask him to take the hurt and the pain away and fill that empty space with his LOVE and Forgiveness.

Josh: You're right…I've been carrying this for too long.

"Father God, thank you for having a plan for me. Thank you for sending Mr. Forbes to guide me in the right direction. I bring my Dad to you, and I let go of the Rejection,

Hurt, Pain, Sadness, Depression, and Fear, and I forgive him, Lord. Maybe he was afraid, maybe he didn't know how to be a Father, maybe he didn't know you, Lord. I pray that you bless him and keep him safe. Let him come to the knowledge of the truth and surrender his life over to you! I no longer have Unforgiveness in my heart. Thank you for filling my heart with your Love and your Peace. I am FREE! In Jesus name Amen!"

Mr. Forbes: That is great, Josh!!! Now...watch what God does!

Josh: Thank you, sir...It is an honor to know you!

Mr. Forbes: It's all God, my friend! The same God that lives in me is the same God that lives in you!
Alright class is over; let's get out of here...My wife is probably wondering what's taking me so long.
You coming over for dinner?

Josh: Sure!

Mr. Forbes: Well, come on then.

Josh: I'll meet you in the front, Mr. Forbes; I have to grab my bag.

Mr. Forbes: Ok, cool.

Josh: (grabs his bag and looks up)

Thank you, Lord! I trust you with my life.

The End